Callie the Cat
A Halloween Story
by Lori Kaiser
Illustrated by Shelbea Combs

Another great book in the Xavier Series!

Published by
Carpe Diem Publishers
17401 Betty Blvd.
Canyon, TX 79015
806-433-6321

www.carpediempublishers.com

© Copyright, 2009 by Carpe Diem Publishers. All Rights Reserved. No portion of this book may be reproduced, stored in a retrieval system, or transmitted, in any form or by any means, electronic, mechanical, photocopying, recording, or otherwise without prior written permission from publisher.
Printed in the United States of America
ISBN 0-9778968-2-X

To my daughter Karson,
I am so proud of you.
God answered my prayers
when he gave me you.

Callie was a little black cat

**who was scared of everything,
this and that.**

She was six weeks old
and lived inside,
but knew very soon
there would come a time:

She would be adopted
and have a new home.

She wished there was a way to know.

There was only one question that gave Callie a fright:

Would she be adopted on Halloween night?

Now Callie, she was a smart little cat,

and knew witches wanted cats that were black.

They were ugly and scary with faces all green.

Callie was frightened
by the horrible sight;
Scary creatures came out
on Halloween night.

Callie looked up and saw a sweet girl

www.ingramcontent.com/pod-product-compliance
Lightning Source LLC
Chambersburg PA
CBHW042045290426
44109CB00001B/35